ENCLOSURESTUDIES
FORJAZZVIOLIN

A Complete Guide to The Art of Jazz Soloing With Diatonic & Chromatic Enclosures

MATT**HOLBORN**

FUNDAMENTAL**CHANGES**

Enclosure Studies For Jazz Violin

A Complete Guide to The Art of Jazz Soloing With Diatonic & Chromatic Enclosures

ISBN: 978-1-78933-450-0

Published by www.fundamental-changes.com

Copyright © 2024 Matt Holborn

Edited by Joseph Alexander

The moral right of this author has been asserted.

All rights reserved. No part of this publication may be reproduced, stored in a retrieval system, or transmitted in any form or by any means, without the prior permission in writing from the publisher.

The publisher is not responsible for websites (or their content) that are not owned by the publisher.

www.fundamental-changes.com

For over 350 free guitar lessons with videos check out:

www.fundamental-changes.com

Join our free Facebook Community of Cool Musicians

www.facebook.com/groups/fundamentalguitar

Tag us for a share on Instagram: **FundamentalChanges**

Cover Image Copyright: Ben Danzig, used with permission

@thelens.ofben

Contents

About the Author 4

Introduction 5

Get the Audio 7

How to Use this Book 8

The Fundamental Exercise 9

Chapter One: Approach Notes One Scale Step Above 10

Chapter Two: Approach Notes One Semitone Below 13

Chapter Three: Over-Under Enclosures 18

Chapter Four: Under-Over Enclosures 22

Chapter Five: Pivot Enclosures 26

Chapter Six: Climbing Enclosure One 34

Chapter Seven: Climbing Enclosure Two 38

Chapter Eight: Climbing Enclosure Three 42

Chapter Nine: 3rds, Triads, 7ths, and 9ths 45

Chapter Ten: Complex/Fully Chromatic Enclosures 51

Chapter Eleven: Parker Enclosures 53

Chapter Twelve: Bebop Enclosures 58

Chapter Thirteen: Three Solo Etudes 64

Conclusion 68

About the Author

Matt Holborn is a jazz violinist, composer and teacher based in London.

Hull-born and Scotland-raised, Matt has made London his home for over a decade while establishing himself as a prominent figure in the UK jazz scene.

As a composer, he has worked with The Oxford Philharmonic Orchestra, Domenico Angarano, and Hull Jazz Festival, among others. His compositions have also featured at events like the Spitalfields Music Festival.

Matt has showcased his talent at major venues and festivals including the Festival Django Reinhardt in Fontainebleau, Ronnie Scott's, Pizza Express Jazz Club, London Jazz Festival, and The Queen Elizabeth Hall.

He collaborates with the jazz education organization Tomorrow's Warriors, runs The Jazz Violin Podcast, and teaches aspiring jazz violinists through a unique online platform on Patreon.

Find out more at **www.patreon.com/mattholborn**

Introduction

As a violinist learning to play jazz, you might sometimes feel somewhat isolated. Violinists remain a rarity in the jazz world, and this is reflected in the scarce educational resources tailored specifically for them. This book is designed to be a valuable resource for *you* in the field of jazz violin education.

It aims to target violin students who feel stuck in their jazz studies and is ideal for someone perhaps with some theoretical knowledge and an awareness of soloing on jazz standards, but who is looking to enrich their improvisations with the chromatic and melodic ideas they hear in recordings.

If you're asking…

- How can I make my playing sound more like authentic jazz?
- How can I incorporate more bebop-style chromaticism into my performances?
- What are the notes I hear in jazz solos that don't seem to fit into a specific scale?

…the answer often lies in understanding and using *enclosures*.

Enclosures are a technique used by jazz musicians to decorate and target certain notes when playing a melody or a solo. They add chromatic notes (notes that don't belong to the key of the piece) to jazz, swing, and bebop lines by surrounding a target note to enhance the melody.

This book teaches you to understand, practice, and quickly *play* enclosures in your solos to become a creative, authentic jazz musician. You'll learn to integrate them into your playing and make them an intrinsic part of your musical vocabulary.

Enclosures are heard in jazz from the swing era, through bebop, and into contemporary jazz and form a great deal of the soloing language you hear. The most common forms of these enclosures are explored in this book, and the techniques and language you'll learn are applicable across all styles of jazz and fusion.

Incorporating enclosures into your playing is broken down into easy, manageable steps.

- Each enclosure is introduced with a concise explanation of its construction
- You'll learn how to apply the enclosure while focusing on the violin-friendly key of G Major
- Next, you'll learn the enclosure around all the arpeggios of the major scale, to help you hear and use these enclosures musically, and in context
- You'll then learn licks built from the enclosure for a real-world application of the idea that you can use immediately in your solos
- Finally, you'll learn solos over the chord sequences of famous jazz tunes to place these enclosures in an even more musical context

Violinists often come from musical backgrounds where improvisation isn't emphasized, so here you'll also learn how to practice like a jazz musician by adopting the improvisational practice strategies used by seasoned jazz players.

This book offers two important outcomes for the aspiring jazz violinist:

1. To help you use straightforward exercises to master the sound and application of enclosures and chromatic approaches.

2. To give you a clear practice roadmap, which an improving jazz musician might use to apply this material in a musical way.

Get the Audio

The audio files for this book are available to download for free from www.fundamental-changes.com. The link is in the top right-hand corner. Click on the Strings link then simply select this book title from the drop-down menu and follow the instructions to get the audio.

We recommend that you download the files directly to your computer, not to your tablet, and extract them there before that adds them to your media library.

For over 350 free guitar lessons with videos check out:

www.fundamental-changes.com

Join our free Facebook Community of Cool Musicians

www.facebook.com/groups/fundamentalguitar

Tag us for a share on Instagram: **FundamentalChanges**

How to Use this Book

Designed as a progressive workbook, the ideas here should be tackled sequentially from start to finish, to build your understanding and expand the ideas you are able to hear and play. Once completed, it will also serve as a valuable reference of note enclosures that you can continually revisit to enhance your practice. I still find myself revisiting these exercises in various ways at least once a week.

The book uses G Major for all examples and exercises, because this is relatively simple for violinists and a popular key in various styles of music. This familiarity will allow you to focus on learning the concepts rather than struggling with tricky fingerings.

All the material is centred around the first position on the violin. This is where many violinists feel most at home and find it easiest to express themselves spontaneously. By focusing on this position, you can play with confidence and focus fully on the musical ideas rather than your technique.

I've kept technical challenges to a minimum to ensure the ideas are accessible to a broad range of violinists. By simplifying the technical aspects, you can concentrate more on the enclosures and their musical applications.

Start at the beginning and progress slowly through each example. It's crucial to play through each piece several times until you're comfortable with it, then begin to wean yourself off the written page as soon as possible. This practice will help deepen your understanding and aid in memorization, making it easier to apply these concepts spontaneously when you play.

Be mindful of specific instructions throughout the book, such as when to expand the exercises across the rest of first position, or to apply the techniques to the fundamental key arpeggio exercise. These directions will help you develop an internalised grasp of the material and ensure it resonates musically and technically under your fingers. There's a reason that not all the notes are written out in all exercises. Figuring some things out yourself will quickly make you a much better musician.

Use the audio examples provided to ensure you're hearing and playing the nuances of each enclosure. Start by playing along with the recordings to get a feel for the rhythm and style, then practice independently to solidify your understanding. Once you're confident, challenge yourself by working with a metronome to speed up, and by transposing these concepts to different keys.

Take your time to fully absorb each concept before moving on. If a particular section or chapter feels challenging, remain with it for several practice sessions until you feel you have mastered the content. This book isn't just about learning note enclosures – it's about transforming the way you approach and understand music. It's as much about teaching your ears the melodic options that will start to come out naturally in your solos through your fingers. This takes time and practice, though.

By integrating these practices into your daily routine and combining them with other studies, like learning jazz standards, transcribing solos, and improvising over backing tracks, you'll enrich your musicality and improvisational skills substantially. Remember, the goal is not just to move through the book quickly, but to truly understand and internalize each concept.

The Fundamental Exercise

Many of the exercises in this book are based around an exercise that outlines all the arpeggios in the key of G Major, linking them together in first position with additional scale tones to seamlessly fit into a 4/4 groove. Playing arpeggios based off every degree of the G Major scale results in some chords being repeated as we extend beyond the first octave, however you will quickly learn to play, hear, and internalise the sound of each enclosure and use it naturally in your playing.

As you play through the exercise, try to identify and be aware of the chord being outlined in each bar, as this will enhance your understanding and connection to the scale's structure and application.

Example 0:

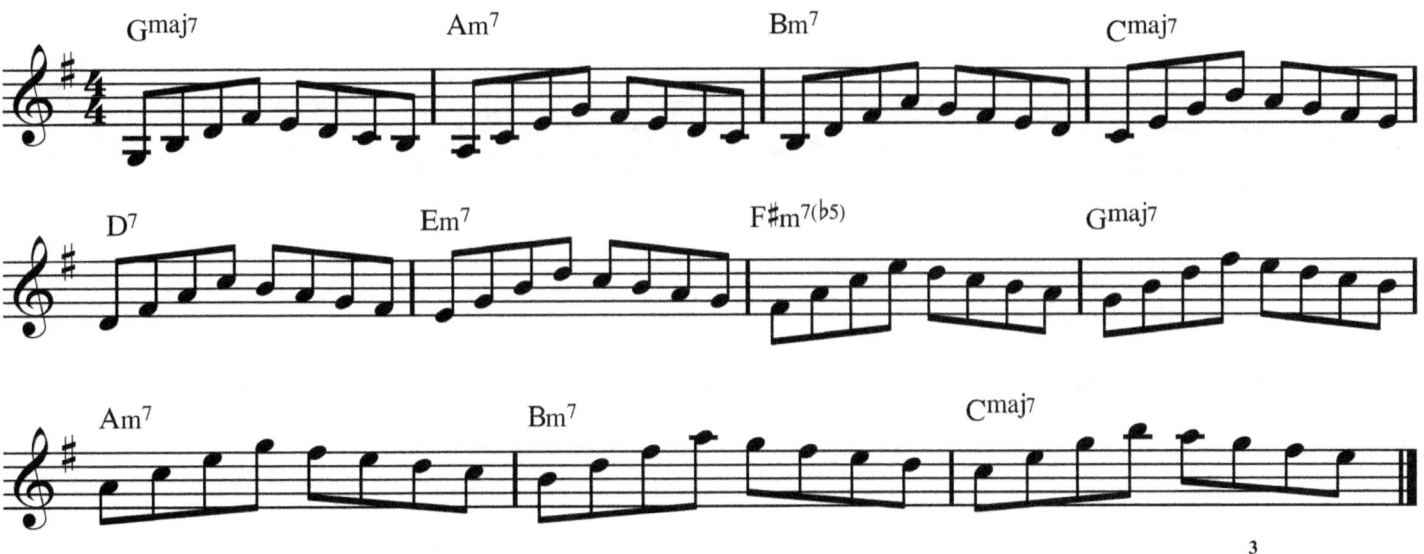

This exercise should be practiced extensively whenever it occurs in the book, and you will be asked to apply each enclosure pattern to its structure.

Don't worry, it will be shown throughout, but you will be asked to take those ideas and run with them, so you need to know this exercise inside out. Reach a point where you can not only play it fluently, but also recall the chords outlined in each section of the exercise.

This practice is invaluable as it helps you to harmonically map out the arpeggios of the major scale, giving you a deeper understanding of its structure and how it relates to real-world chord progressions.

By integrating it into your practice routine, you'll gain a better grasp of how these chords provide both harmonic and melodic foundations for the note enclosures and other improvisational techniques we discuss. This approach ensures that the knowledge you discover is related to its practical, musical applications and improves your ability to create music spontaneously and with greater understanding.

Chapter One: Approach Notes One Scale Step Above

The term "approach notes" describes the notes we use to build enclosures. The simplest form of enclosure is one that involves an approach note directly above the target note, selected from within the scale or key centre in use. As you delve into this book, you'll frequently find that many enclosures include a note above the target note, typically following this arrangement.

Try playing the following exercise a few times. It applies the concept of approach notes to each note of the G Major scale and covers the entire range of first position on the violin, rather than limiting itself to a simple root-to-root progression.

Notice how this exercise might make it seem like you are ascending in major 3rds.

Example 1a

Now, let's reverse the direction.

This time, the exercise involves descending the scale from the top to the bottom of first position.

Example 1b

Next, adjust the rhythm.

Here, the rhythm of our initial example has been slightly altered to place the target note on the beat, rather than the off-beat. This small change creates quite a different musical effect, even though the notes are the same.

Example 1c

Now apply this concept as you move down the scale, similar to the exercise in Example 1b. These exercises may seem straightforward, but they are crucial in beginning to understand more complex enclosures. When applied within simple scale and arpeggio patterns, they start to form a melody.

Use the key arpeggio exercise (Exercise 0) from a couple of pages ago, and integrate our newly acquired approach note enclosure.

Example 1d

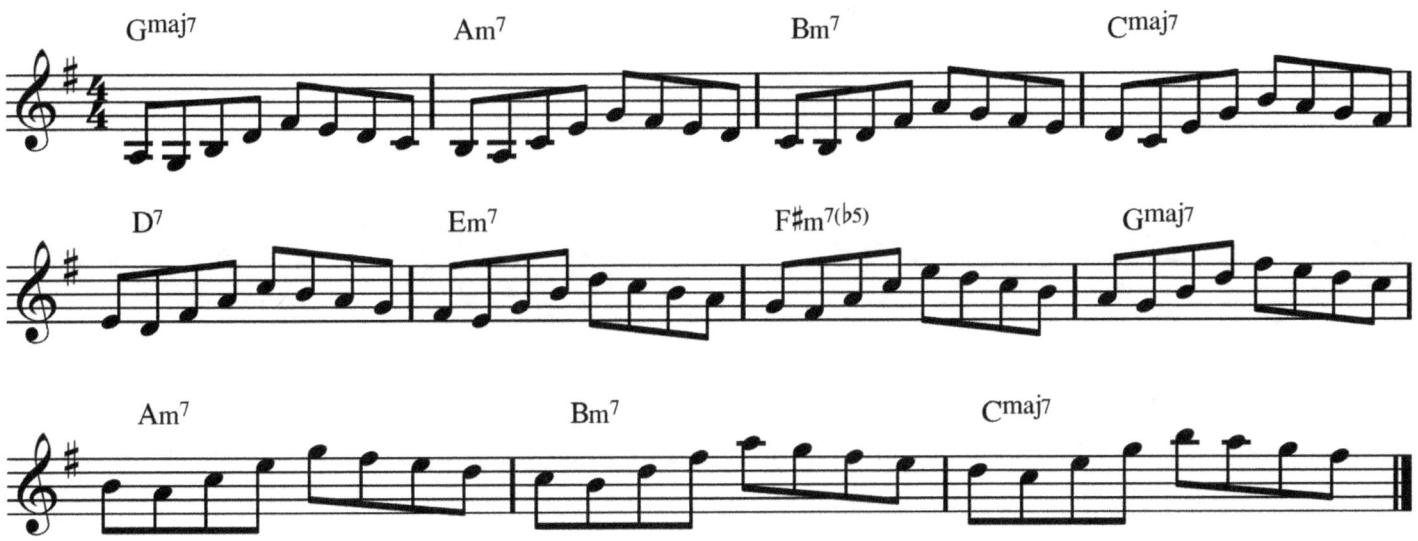

This exercise uses the same concept as the previous one but in reverse. It's slightly more difficult on the way down due to the larger intervals at the end of each bar.

Example 1e

As you progress through this book, I will encourage you to take more initiative in extending these exercises beyond one octave to explore more of first position. This approach will not only deepen your understanding of the violin's fretboard, but enhance your ability to creatively apply music theory to practical playing.

Musical Lines and Ideas

Try the exercise below, which incorporates the enclosure technique across all the notes of the G major arpeggio. In the first two bars, the approach note falls on the beat, while in the following two bars, the line shifts by half a beat, aligning the target note with the beat.

Example 1f:

Here's a straightforward line applying this concept over a ii-V-I progression in G major. Notice the enclosure highlighted within the box.

Example 1g:

Chapter Two: Approach Notes One Semitone Below

Approaching a target note from a semitone below is a widely used idea and an integral part of most enclosures. They are nearly universal in their application. Familiarizing yourself with their sound and mastering their execution is an excellent first step towards incorporating chromatic details into your playing.

The exercises below demonstrate the "semitone below" approach note on every note of the major scale. This is a quick way to hear and understand the chromatic idea, while exploring the major scale in a way you might not have considered before.

Play the following exercise a few times. Finish by extending the pattern up to the top of first position, where you enclose the notes A and B on the E string. Below, I've suggested some fingerings that I find effective.

Example 2a:

Now, play Exercise 2b below, this time descending the G Major scale using the same concept.

Example 2b:

Once you're comfortable with the two exercises above, combine them. Using the same rhythm and covering all of first position, start by enclosing the A on the G string and finish by enclosing the B on the E string.

Now, move on to the exercise below. This one extends halfway up first position with a continuous rhythm, featuring no rests between the approach notes.

Although more challenging, this exercise is highly beneficial as both a technical drill and a way to practice chromatically targeting notes from the major scale.

Example 2c:

The next exercise incorporates our key arpeggio exercise, along with our newly learned simple approach note. I've added chord symbols above the blank bars for reference.

Example 2d:

Next, try reversing the process just as we did with the previous exercise. Start from the highest point in first position and work your way down. Here's a hint for how to proceed...

Example 2e:

Musical Lines and Ideas

Here are some practical uses for this simple approach note. The following example showcases a line that fits over a ii-V-I progression, including the enclosure of the 3rd and the root of the D7 chord.

Example 2f:

This example also works well over a ii-V-I progression, approaching the root of the Am7 chord, the 3rd of the D7 chord, and the 3rd of the G major chord.

Example 2g:

The next example functions over a I-vi-ii-V sequence. It approaches the 3rd of G major and the root of Am7.

Example 2h:

The next two examples are quite similar. They cover the range of first position while approaching each of the chord tones of a G major triad and an E minor triad.

Example 2i:

Example 2j:

Here's an example that fits over a static major 7th chord. It could work over any type of major chord, but it specifically uses the 7th, 5th, and 3rd of the chord prominently.

Example 2k:

The next example works over a static minor 7th chord, approaching the root of the chord.

Example 2l:

Finally, here is an etude that uses a straightforward set of chord changes in the key of G Major. The sequence closely resembles the A section of tunes like *Honeysuckle Rose* and *Scrapple from the Apple*.

Example 2m:

The two approach notes we've explored so far are foundational building blocks for playing enclosures and a simple way to add chromaticism to any phrase. It seems that most people prefer hearing chromatic approaches from below, and hearing the scale step from above also feels quite natural. This is a pattern that recurs throughout this book and is commonly observed in jazz and other music genres.

While this is a rule that's often used, however, it's also frequently broken, and we'll be doing just that by the end of the book. But, it's beneficial to grasp it as an important fundamental concept.

Chapter Three: Over-Under Enclosures

If we combine the two approach notes from chapters one and two, then we create one of the most common enclosures in jazz, which I call the "over-under enclosure". This is where we play a scale step above the target note, then a semitone below it.

The result is a very strong melodic pattern, and once you have worked on it, you will start to notice it everywhere.

The first example applies this enclosure to first position.

Example 3a:

Try the descending version below and extend the exercise using the rest of first position.

Example 3b:

Now let's ascend in continuous 1/4 notes using the enclosures to decorate the notes. You may notice that this becomes groups of three 1/8th notes over 4/4, which creates an interesting cross-rhythmic effect. Extend this exercise using the rest of first position and apply it to the descending sequence.

Example 3c:

Now it's time to apply the pattern to our key arpeggio exercise in G Major. I've started you off, but I want you to continue the exercise on your own. It's the best way to learn.

Example 3d:

Musical Lines and Ideas

The example below is played over a ii-V-I progression. It encloses the 5th of Am7 and the root note of G major.

Example 3e:

The next example is a line over a V-I sequence. It encloses the 3rd of D7 and both the 3rd and root of G major 7.

Example 3f:

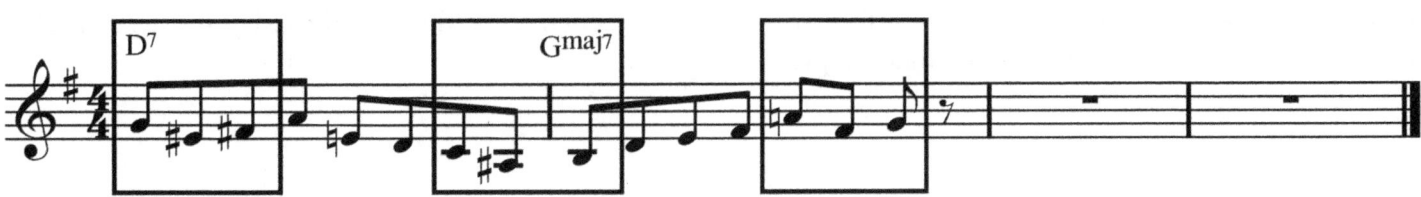

The following example works over a I-vi-ii-V sequence. It encloses the 5th of G major, the 9th of Am7, and the root of D7. It then moves to enclose the root of Em7 and continues enclosing the major scale up to the note of G.

Example 3g:

The next two examples are quite similar. They span the range of first position, enclosing each of the chord tones of a G major triad and an E minor triad.

Example 3h:

Example 3i:

Lastly, here's an etude that uses a straightforward set of chord changes in the key of G Major. This sequence is reminiscent of the A section of the tune *Coquette*.

Example 3j:

21

Chapter Four: Under-Over Enclosures

This enclosure is created by playing a semitone below a target note and a scale tone above – the mirror image of the enclosure we looked at in the previous chapter.

Although they sound similar, playing them consecutively highlights their differences. Thinking of them as distinct sounds will add depth to your playing. This approach marks the beginning of building a repertoire of enclosures for your ears and fingers to utilize when playing over jazz standards.

The exercise below applies the enclosure to the lowest six notes in first position in the key of G Major.

Example 4a:

Now descend the sequence shown below. After practicing, extend this exercise using the rest of first position.

Example 4b:

Next, play this version ascending with continuous 1/8th notes. Notice that this results in groups of three 1/8th notes over a 4/4 time signature. Extend this exercise using the rest of first position.

Example 4c:

Example 4d:

Combine this exercise with the arpeggio exercise and our newly mastered enclosure technique.

Musical Lines and Ideas

Below are some ways to implement this simple enclosure. Experiment with these examples alongside full recordings and then with backing-only tracks.

This line encloses the 5th of the Am7.

Example 4e:

This line encloses the 3rd of the Am7 and both the 7th and 3rd of the D7.

Example 4f:

This line encloses the 3rd of G major, the root of Am7, and the root of G major.

Example 4g:

The following two examples cover the range of first position, enclosing each of the chord tones of G and C major triads.

Example 4h:

Example 4i:

Here's an etude set over some straightforward chord changes in the key of G Major. The sequence is a lot like the A section of the popular tune *My Heart Stood Still*. Even though we're in the key of G Major, you'll notice a few chords that don't usually pop up in the G Major scale. However, the lines do stick to the G Major scale. Playing in this way can help create a very coherent sense of melody.

Example 4j:

25

Chapter Five: Pivot Enclosures

Pivot enclosures are so called because they "pivot" around the target note before landing on it, allowing us to hear the target note inside the enclosure.

These enclosures create a feeling of suspense and often sound great at the start or end of a phrase, where they can either delay the beginning, or delay the resolution, of a melody. I've included four of the most common ones in this chapter.

Let's learn these movements and apply them to the major scale and our key arpeggio exercise.

Pivot 1

This enclosure starts on the target note, moves down a semitone, up a scale step, down again, and then lands back on the target note.

Work through the example below, which uses the first pivot enclosure on the lowest seven notes in first position in the key of G Major.

Example 5a:

Play the example below, starting from the top and descending through the sequence. Try extending this exercise to include the rest of first position.

Example 5b:

Now, combine this pattern with the key arpeggio exercise using our newly learned enclosure technique. Make sure to complete the exercise all the way through first position.

Example 5c:

Notice that this exercise is played in 6/8 time, as that rhythm suits the enclosure well and organises the notes into groups of six.

Pivot 2

This pivot enclosure is similar to Pivot 1 but with a small tweak. Instead of going below the note twice, this version goes *above* the note twice, still following the same rules of moving above by a scale step and below by a semitone.

Even these small changes in how you play enclosures can make them sound different and give your playing a distinct feel. As you explore more of these enclosures, you'll likely start to have your favourites. These choices will become part of your personal musical vocabulary and help shape your unique sound.

Example 5d:

Extend this exercise by playing through the rest of first position. Once you reach the top, try descending back down.

Example 5e:

Note that this exercise is a condensed version of the previous one, but now in 4/4 time.

This variation demonstrates the flexibility and possibilities that these enclosures and exercises offer. Feel free to experiment. Try swapping them around, converting the previous exercise to 4/4 time, or adapting this one to fit into 6/8. This kind of practice not only builds your technique but also expands your creative approach.

Pivot 3

This pivot creates a particularly melodic sound. It starts with a scale step above the target note, moves to the target note, drops a semitone below, then lands back on the target note.

Try the example below. This enclosure is applied to the major scale. Make sure to continue the exercise through the rest of first position and also play it descending once you reach the top.

Example 5f:

The example below follows a similar pattern to the previous one but flows continuously without any breaks, creating a very melodic sound. This could easily be used as a melodic device in your solos, just as it is.

Example 5g:

The example below takes the same concept but descends from the top of first position.

Example 5h:

Next, play the following exercise, which combines the key arpeggio exercise with our newly acquired enclosure technique.

Example 5i:

Pivot 4

This enclosure is similar to Pivot 3 but includes an additional movement above the target note before finally resting on it.

Now, play the example below. This enclosure is applied to the major scale. Be sure to continue the exercise through the rest of first position, and also play it descending once you reach the top.

Example 5j:

Now play the exercise below, which integrates the key arpeggio exercise with our newly learned enclosure. Complete the exercise by extending it through the rest of first position.

Example 5k:

Musical Lines and Ideas

Here are some practical examples of how you can use different pivot enclosures over a ii-V-I sequence and static chords.

The line below utilizes Pivot 1 over a ii-V-I sequence, enclosing the root of A minor and the 5th of G major.

Example 5l:

This next line applies Pivot 2 over a ii-V-I sequence, enclosing the 3rd of D7 and the 3rd of G major.

Example 5m:

The following line features Pivot 3 over a ii-V-I sequence, using the enclosure to ascend the scale from D to F#.

Example 5n:

The line below uses Pivot 4 over a ii-V-I sequence, enclosing the root of A Minor 7.

Example 5o:

These lines are played over static chord vamps.

This line uses Pivot 1 over a static G major chord, staying in one region of the instrument.

Example 5p:

The next line applies Pivot 2 over a C major chord, also focusing on a specific area on the fretboard.

Example 5q:

The following two lines use pivot enclosures over static E minor chords, both focusing on the same area of the instrument.

This line uses Pivot 3 over an E minor chord.

Example 5r:

This line applies Pivot 4 over an E minor chord.

Example 5s:

This line combines Pivot 1 and Pivot 4 over a ii-V-I sequence.

Example 5t:

This line integrates Pivot 2 and Pivot 3 over a ii-V-I sequence.

Example 5u:

Finally, this etude incorporates all four pivot enclosures and is structured around some simple chord changes typical of a tune in the key of G Major.

Example 5v:

Chapter Six: Climbing Enclosure One

There are three types of enclosures I classify as "climbing enclosures". Each one involves going either above or below the target note by a tone, then climbing up or down to reach that target note. These are very common and melodic enclosures that will add some real spice to your lines.

This first enclosure starts a scale step above the target note, drops below it by a tone, then climbs up to the target note chromatically.

Play through the example below, which applies this enclosure to the major scale. In this instance, I have made the target note longer to highlight it.

Example 6a

Now play the example below, but this time do not hold the target note. This turns it into a nice melodic device that can work well in various musical contexts.

Example 6b

Now play the example below, which features the same enclosure but descending the scale.

Example 6c:

To make this exercise a bit more interesting on the way down, try removing the last note in each sequence. This eliminates the doubled note and makes each sequence flow smoothly into the next.

Example 6d:

The exercise above, either in whole or in part, can be used as an intriguing line. You'll often hear fragments of this scalic pattern in iconic jazz solos.

Notice that removing the doubled note turns this into a three-note sequence, which rhythmically consists of three 1/4 notes. When played in 4/4 this creates a nice polyrhythmic effect.

Now, proceed with the exercise below, integrating the key arpeggio exercise with our newly learned enclosure. Make sure to complete the exercise through the rest of first position.

Example 6e

Musical Lines and Ideas

Here are some practical ways to use the enclosure in different musical contexts.

This line uses the enclosure over a G major chord, moving from root to root.

Example 6f:

The next line applies the enclosure over an E minor chord, also from root to root.

Example 6g:

This line uses the enclosure over a ii-V-I sequence.

Example 6h:

Here's another application of the enclosure over a ii-V-I sequence.

Example 6i:

This line uses the enclosure over a I-vi-ii-V sequence.

Example 6j:

Finally, this line uses the enclosure over a repeating I-vi-ii-V sequence.

Example 6k:

Chapter Seven: Climbing Enclosure Two

This enclosure is similar to the one in the previous chapter, but mixes up the movements and introduces a small change to one of the notes below the target.

It begins on the scale step below the target note, climbs up to the scale step above the target, then drops back down below the target note, this time a full tone below. While this often corresponds to a scale step, there are instances where it might not. From there, it climbs up chromatically from the tone below straight to the target note. Though this might sound complex, in practice you'll hear that it creates a pleasing, melodic bluesy effect.

Play the example below that applies this enclosure to the major scale. Once you are comfortable, extend this exercise to include the rest of first position.

Example 7a

Now play the sequence descending. Extend this exercise using the rest of first position.

Example 7b

Try playing the sequence ascending again, but this time omit the last note. You'll notice that the last note of the sequence when ascending is the same as the first note of the next sequence. By omitting this doubled note, you create a smoother transition up the scale, weaving an interesting melody. Once you're comfortable with this pattern, extend the exercise to include the rest of first position.

Example 7c

Now, try this exercise by combining it with the key arpeggio exercise and our newly introduced enclosure. Make sure to carry on with the exercise through the rest of first position.

Example 7d:

This next exercise is an expanded version of the previous one. Extend it across the entire first position. Once you reach the top, experiment with descending to explore how it sounds moving in reverse.

Example 7e:

Exploring different variations of these exercises is an excellent way to apply them in diverse musical situations and uncover new approaches to navigating the scales.

Musical Lines and Ideas

This line applies the enclosure technique to a static G major chord, enclosing the 3rd before climbing up the chord.

Example 7f:

This line applies the enclosure to a static E minor chord, encloses the 5th, and then climbs up the chord.

Example 7g:

40

This line is set over a ii-V-I progression. It encloses the 5th of Am7 and the 3rd of the G major chord. Note that the enclosure starts just before the G chord is played.

Example 7h:

This line is also performed over a ii-V-I progression. It weaves around the Am7 chord before enclosing the 9th of the D7 chord.

Example 7i:

This line is played over a I-vi-ii-V-i progression. It encloses the fifth of the E minor chord, then the 3rd of the Am7 chord.

Example 7j

This line is played over a I-vi-ii-V progression. It encloses the root of the G major chord, the 5th of the Em7 chord, then the 9th and the 3rd of the Am7 chord, and finally the root of the D7 chord.

Example 7k

Chapter Eight: Climbing Enclosure Three

This enclosure reaches above the target note by a diatonic 3rd, moves up by a tone, then descends chromatically to the target. It can sound particularly appealing when targeting the root of the chord you are playing over.

Example 8a:

Extend this exercise through the rest of first position. In this case, focus on applying it to the lower end of the position. I suggest starting from the top and descending beyond the section of the sequence I've written here.

Now, integrate this exercise with the key arpeggio exercise and our newly learned enclosure. Extend this exercise to cover the entire first position. Once you reach the top, try descending to explore how it sounds moving in reverse.

Example 8b

Musical Lines and Ideas

This line uses the enclosure over a static G major chord, enclosing the 5th.

Example 8c

This line applies the enclosure to a static E minor chord, enclosing the root.

Example 8d

This line is played over a ii-V-I progression, enclosing the root of the Am7.

Example 8e

This line is also over a ii-V-I, enclosing the 7th of the Am7.

Example 8f

This line is played over a repeating I-vi-ii-V progression, enclosing the 5th of the E minor chord then, right at the end, the 7th of the Am7 chord.

Example 8g

This line follows a I-vi-ii-V progression as well, enclosing the root of G major and then, towards the end, the 7th of the D7 chord.

Example 8h

This etude uses all three climbing enclosures over some simple chord changes.

Example 8i

Chapter Nine: 3rds, Triads, 7ths, and 9ths

These are some of my favourite melodic and rhythmic devices, each one building on the previous idea. Mastering these will equip you with a versatile set of melodic tools that you can apply in a variety of musical contexts.

All these devices originate from the first chromatic approach note we explored at the beginning of the book, approaching a target note from underneath by a semitone.

Jazz 3rds

This is the simplest of these melodic devices. We approach our target note from underneath by a semitone, then move down the scale by a 3rd.

Play the example below, which applies the concept to the major scale.

Example 9a

Now, work this out starting from the bottom of first position and ascending. I've given you a start below.

Example 9b

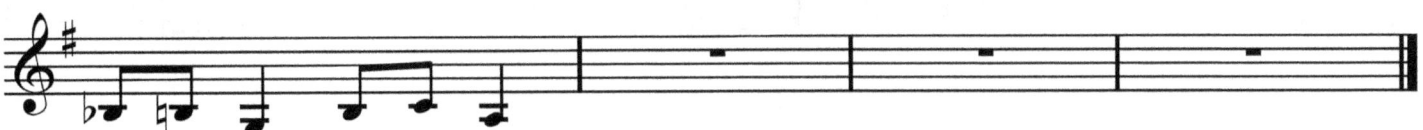

Triads

By adding another 3rd below our initial note, we create a more complex sound that forms a root position triad, with the root being the bottom note of the triad. This is a highly melodic idea that fits well in most musical contexts within the key of G Major. You'll often hear musicians like Stan Getz using this concept in their playing.

Example 9c

I prefer the sound of it descending, as shown in the example below. Once again, extend this exercise by descending to the bottom of first position.

Example 9d

7ths

By adding another 3rd, we form 7th chords, which are triads with their 7ths added at the top. We touched on some four-note chords at the beginning of the book, but here they are enhanced with a nice chromatic enclosure.

Example 9e

Play this pattern through first position. Once you reach the top, continue by playing the pattern as you descend the scale.

9ths

Here we add a 9th near the bottom of the chord between the 3rd and the root. It creates this super melodic variation.

Example 9f

Again, play this pattern through the entire first position. Once you reach the top, begin to play the pattern as you descend the scale.

Combination Exercise

This exercise serves as an example of how you can utilise variations and combinations of the above melodic devices to create interesting exercises that challenge your brain, fingers, and understanding of scales.

Example 9g

This combination exercise melds jazz triads and jazz 9ths, offering a dynamic approach to the concepts we've learned.

Musical Lines and Ideas

Here are a few lines that utilize this combined device.

This line applies the enclosure to a static G major chord, enclosing the 5th.

Example 9h:

This line applies the enclosure to a static E minor chord, enclosing the 5th and the 4th.

Example 9i:

This line is played over a ii-V-I progression. It encloses the 9th of the Am7, the 5th of the D7, and the root of the G major.

Example 9j:

This line is played over a ii-V-I progression. It encloses the 7th of the Am7, the 3rd and the 9th of the D7, and the 5th and the 3rd of the G major.

Example 9k

This line is played over a I-vi-ii-V-i progression. It encloses the 3rd of the G major, the 5th of the Em7, and the 4th of the Am7.

Example 9l:

Another line over a I-vi-ii-V progression encloses the 5th of the Em7 and the 5th of the D7.

Example 9m:

Now learn this etude which incorporates 3rds, triads, 7ths, and 9ths over a straightforward chord sequence.

Example 9n:

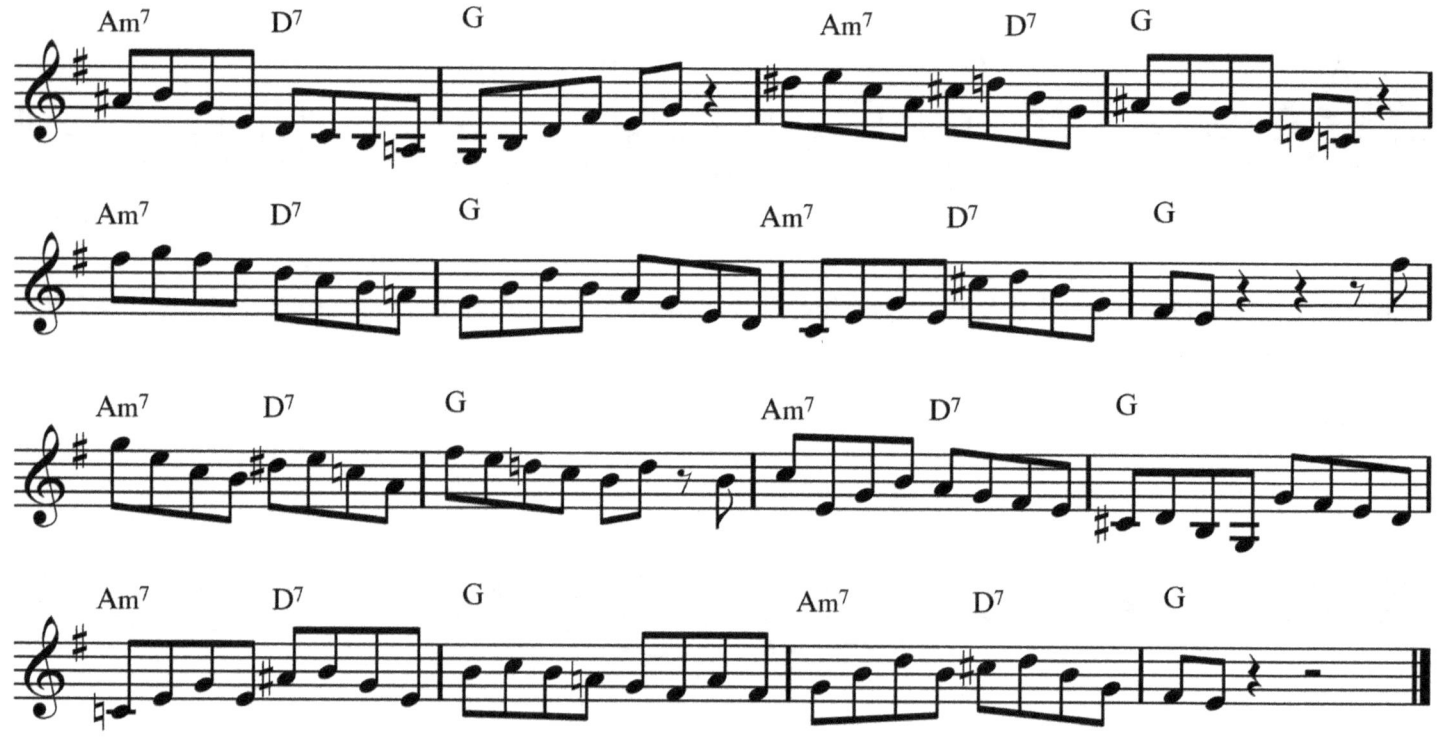

50

Chapter Ten: Complex/Fully Chromatic Enclosures

This final section explores some of the more chromatic and non-diatonic enclosures that are prevalent in bebop music. Many of the techniques discussed here can be heard in the playing of Charlie Parker, and you'll also find them in later swing music, such as the performances of Oscar Peterson.

Unlike earlier examples, where we often ascended by a scale step when going above the target note, the enclosures in this last section diverge from that pattern. All the enclosures here are fully chromatic, meaning that they don't relate to the key centre we're playing in.

Chromatic Above and Below

Let's start with an introductory enclosure. If you've worked diligently through the previous chapters, this concept will be easier to grasp.

In this enclosure, we approach the target note by moving a semitone above and below it.

This approach can add a rich layer of complexity to your playing, making your lines sound more intricate and nuanced. As you practice, try applying this chromatic enclosure to both the major scale and our key arpeggio exercise, to see how it enhances your musical expression.

Example 10a

Now, try playing this example using our new enclosure applied to our key arpeggio exercise.

Example 10b:

Next, apply this enclosure to a ii-V-I lick to see how it alters the feel and complexity of the line.

Example 10c:

Now try this lick over a I-vi-ii-V-I sequence, which uses the same chromatic enclosure technique.

Example 10d:

The above examples might be a bit more challenging to grasp both mentally and aurally, compared to earlier examples in the book which were based on the major scale. However, with consistent practice and attentive listening, it is definitely possible to become comfortable with these concepts. Now, let's move on to some of the more complicated chromatic enclosures.

Chapter Eleven: Parker Enclosures

These enclosures are named after Charlie Parker because you can frequently hear him using them in his playing. They have since become a staple in the toolkits of most jazz musicians.

Parker Enclosure 1

This enclosure begins on the target note, moves up a tone, drops down a semitone, goes below the target note by a semitone, then lands back on the target note.

We'll apply it first to the major scale, then our key arpeggio exercise. Play the exercise below.

Example 11a:

Now, try this exercise that combines the key arpeggio exercise and our newly acquired enclosure.

Example 11b:

Parker Enclosure 2

This enclosure is similar to the first but begins with a semitone below the target note. Play through it now.

Example 11c

This exercise combines our new enclosure with the key arpeggio exercise.

Example 11d

Here are several musical ideas using the Parker enclosures.

The first idea is played over a static G major chord. It uses the Parker 1 enclosure to enclose the root, then moves around the triad, repeating the process for the 3rd and 5th of the chord, and finishes by descending the triad.

Example 11e:

The next idea is executed on a static E minor chord. It begins by enclosing the root with the Parker 2 enclosure, jumps up a 3rd, and repeats this pattern on the 3rd and 5th of the chord before descending the triad to conclude.

Example 11f:

This line is played over a ii-V-I progression. It uses the Parker 1 enclosure to enclose the 3rd of the Am7 chord.

Example 11g:

Another line over a ii-V-I uses the Parker 2 enclosure to enclose the 5th of the Am7 and the root of the G major chord.

Example 11h:

This line is played over a repeating ii-V that moves to the I chord at the end. It pre-emptively uses the Parker 2 enclosure on the 7th of the D7 chord and the 3rd of the G major chord.

Example 11i

This line is played over the same sequence and uses the Parker 2 enclosure on the 5th of Am7.

Example 11j:

This line is played over a I-vi-ii-V sequence. It uses the Parker 1 enclosure on the 3rd of Em7 and then pre-emptively over the 3rd of the D7 chord.

Example 11k:

This line is played over a I-vi-ii-V-I sequence. It pre-emptively uses the Parker 2 enclosure on the 7th of the D7 chord.

Example 11l:

This line is played over a I-vi-ii-V-I sequence. It pre-emptively uses the Parker 1 enclosure on the root of the G major chord.

Example 11m:

This line is played over a I-vi-ii-V-1 sequence and pre-emptively uses the Parker 2 enclosure on the 5th of the Am7 chord.

Example 11n:

Chapter Twelve: Bebop Enclosures

Anyone familiar with jazz from the bebop era onward will recognize this type of enclosure.

This enclosure pattern involves going under the target note by a semitone, above by a tone, down by a semitone, and under by a semitone again before finally landing on the target note. It's quite similar to the previous enclosures, but here we deliberately prolong the moment when we play the target note.

Unlike the Parker enclosures, we don't need to consider what key these ideas are in – our focus is purely on the tones and semitones above and below the target notes, not on any diatonic scale steps.

For this enclosure, I've written it out for most of first position. There's quite a bit to remember, and it might take some time before your ear is able to confidently guide you with this one.

Example 12a

Now that you've worked on ascending with the bebop enclosure, try playing the exercise descending back down the scale. This will help solidify your understanding and ability to apply the enclosure in both directions.

Next, integrate this enclosure with the key arpeggio exercise. Start the combined exercise and, once you reach the top of first position, continue by going back down the scale to complete the exercise.

Example 12b:

Double Bebop Enclosure

This variation is an extension of the basic jazz enclosure but includes an extra note, adding complexity and richness to the pattern. The placement of this extra note is rhythmically crucial. It sounds best starting on the "&" of beat 4, as I have indicated. This positioning not only enhances its musicality but is also essential for capturing the style accurately, as this type of phrasing is prevalent in many jazz recordings. Think of it as an enclosure within an enclosure, which adds a unique twist to the familiar pattern.

Begin by playing this exercise, incorporating it into the major scale and our key arpeggio exercise. Once you reach the top of first position, continue the exercise by descending back down the scale.

Example 12c:

Next, integrate both the bebop enclosure and double bebop enclosure with our trusted arpeggio exercise. Start the exercise and, after completing it through the rest of first position, descend back down the scale to reinforce the technique.

Example 12d:

Musical Lines and Ideas

This first line is played over a static G major chord. It uses the bebop enclosure on the 3rd of the G major chord, then moves around the triad, applying the same enclosure technique on the 5th and the root. This approach not only enhances the melody but also adds a layer of complexity and interest to the overall harmony.

Example 12e

This idea is played over a static E minor chord. It features the double bebop enclosure on the 5th of the E minor chord before darting around the triad and applying the same technique on the root, 3rd, and 5th again, ultimately landing on the root.

Example 12f:

This line is played over a ii-V-I sequence. It uses the jazz enclosure on the 3rd of the Am7.

Example 12g:

This line is executed over a ii-V-I sequence, utilising the double bebop enclosure on the 5th of the D7 chord.

Example 12h:

This line is played over a repeating ii-V sequence that resolves to the I chord at the end. It employs the bebop enclosure to pre-emptively enclose the 3rd of the D7.

Example 12i:

This line, played over the same sequence, uses the double bebop enclosure to pre-emptively enclose the 7th of the D7 chord and then the 9th of the Am7 chord.

Example 12j

This line is played over a I-vi-ii-V-I progression. It uses the bebop enclosure to pre-emptively enclose the root of the Em chord.

Example 12k:

This line is also played over a I-vi-ii-V-I progression. It utilises the double bebop enclosure to pre-emptively enclose the 5th of the Am chord, then the 3rd of the G major chord.

Example 12l:

Another line over a I-vi-ii-V-I sequence employs the bebop enclosure to enclose the 3rd of the Em chord and the 9th of the D7 chord.

Example 12m:

This line, executed over a I-vi-ii-V-I progression, uses the double bebop enclosure to pre-emptively enclose the 7th of the Am chord, then the root of the G major chord.

Example 12n

Finally, this etude integrates all the complex enclosures discussed in this chapter into a straightforward chord sequence. By applying these advanced techniques over a simpler harmonic backdrop, you can focus on the intricacies of each enclosure, refining your ability to execute them fluidly while maintaining musicality.

This approach will not only challenge your technical skills but enhance your understanding of how these enclosures can be woven into various musical contexts to enrich your improvisational vocabulary.

Example 12o

Chapter Thirteen: Three Solo Etudes

Let's conclude with some solos over three common chord progressions, each played in different keys from the material you've studied so far. This variety will encourage you to apply the enclosures and concepts you've learned in new musical contexts, broadening your ability to use them musically.

These solos offer a more real-world application of the ideas explored throughout this book and are crafted to mimic the flow and feel of actual improvisations you might perform on a tune. I encourage you to learn these solos and try to identify where the concepts we've discussed are being used.

This practical application will help cement your understanding and enable you to integrate these techniques seamlessly into your own playing.

1. Rhythm Changes

2. Lady

3. All

Conclusion

Congratulations on reaching the end of this book! By now, I hope you have a solid understanding of what an enclosure is, how to play them on your violin, and how you might integrate them into your own performances.

The exercises, lines, and melodic ideas we've covered continue to inspire me. Whenever I'm unsure what to practice, I turn to material similar to that included in these pages. Sometimes, I use it to focus on a key centre that challenges me, or to develop new lines for difficult chord progressions.

Other times, when learning solos by great musicians, I rely on my knowledge from this book to dissect what I hear and play, enhancing my understanding and technique.

This material can serve as a rich source of practice content for you or your students, just as it has for me. As musicians, I believe it's crucial that we commit to continually deepening our understanding of our instruments and our music throughout our lives. While many jazz violin educational resources cater to beginners, this book is designed to be an encyclopaedic reference for those of us who are lifelong students of jazz.

May it aid you well on your musical journey.

Matt

www.ingramcontent.com/pod-product-compliance
Lightning Source LLC
LaVergne TN
LVHW061255060426
835507LV00020B/2325